Skydiver

Saving the Fastest Bird in the World

Celia Godkin

pajamapress

The author would like to thank Marcel A. Gahbauer of McGill University for his invaluable assistance in checking the scientific accuracy of this book. The Raptors in Duncan, B.C., provided a direct encounter with a wide variety of birds of prey, including peregrine falcons.

First published in the United States in 2014

Text and illustration copyright © Celia Godkin
This edition copyright © 2014 Pajama Press Inc.
This is a first edition.
10 9 8 7 6 5 4 3 2 1

www.pajamapress.ca   info@pajamapress.ca

 Canada Council   Conseil des arts
for the Arts   du Canada

 ONTARIO ARTS COUNCIL
CONSEIL DES ARTS DE L'ONTARIO
50 YEARS OF ONTARIO GOVERNMENT SUPPORT OF THE ARTS
50 ANS DE SOUTIEN DU GOUVERNEMENT DE L'ONTARIO AUX ARTS

The publisher gratefully acknowledges the support of the Canada Council for the Arts and the Ontario Arts Council for its publishing program. We acknowledge the financial support of the Government of Canada through the Canada Book Fund for our publishing activities.

Library and Archives Canada Cataloguing in Publication

Godkin, Celia, author   Skydiver : saving the fastest bird in the world / Celia Godkin.
ISBN 978-1-927485-61-3 (bound)
          1. Peregrine falcon--Juvenile literature. 2. Endangered species-- Juvenile literature. I. Title.
QL696.F34G63 2014   j598.9'6   C2013-908350-2

Publisher Cataloging-in-Publication Data (U.S.)

Godkin, Celia.
    Skydiver : saving the fastest bird in the world / Celia Godkin.
[32] pages : col. ill. ; cm.
Summary: The story of a peregrine falcon and its mate's struggle to raise their young is told against the backdrop of scientists' efforts to understand the raptors' decline in the wild. After a devastating effect on the bird's lifecycle is linked to the pesticide DDT, the world's fastest bird must depend on humans to recover and thrive once more.
ISBN-13: 978-1-927485-61-3
1. Peregrine falcon – Behavior – Juvenile literature. 2. Peregrine falcon – Ecology – Juvenile literature. I. Title.
598.96 dc23 QL696.F34G634 2014

Manufactured by QuaLibre Inc.
Printed in the United States of America

Pajama Press Inc.
112 Berkeley St. Toronto, Ontario Canada, M5A 2W7
Distributed in the US by Orca Book Publishers
PO Box 468 Custer, WA, 98240-0468, USA

This book is for the new clutch: Joshua, Ethan, Noelle, Tariq, and Sophia

It is spring. High in the sky, a peregrine falcon heads north. She flies on and on, until she spots a familiar cliff face. This is her nesting site, where she returns year after year. She descends and lands gently on a rocky ledge near the top.

The peregrine waits patiently for her mate to join her. When her sharp eyes spot his familiar shape, she lets out a welcome cry: "*Witchew, witchew.*"

Wanting to impress the female with his mastery of the skies, the male greets her with a spectacular aerial display. First he flies high in the sky. Then, with breathtaking speed, he plummets toward the earth. No animal on earth travels faster than a diving peregrine.

At the bottom of his dive, he sweeps upward in an exuberant loop-de-loop. The female sees that her mate had lost none of his hunting skills. Joyfully she rises up to join him.

Together, they swoop and tumble in a dazzling courtship dance.

Over the next few days, the female peregrine lays four eggs. They rest in a shallow depression the pair has scraped out on the ledge. While the large female guards the eggs from predators, the smaller male hunts for both of them.

Hovering high over his territory,
the male peregrine spots a
solitary bird. Out of the blue,
he hurtles down on his victim,
killing it the instant they collide.

As the male peregrine carries his prize back to the nest, he spots two people near the top of the cliff. One of them is lowering herself on a rope over the edge. The female peregrine cries out in alarm: "*Cack cack cack cack,*" and flies off to escape the intruder.

The woman moves carefully down the rock face until she is within reach of the eggs. Then, one by one, she places them gently in a special pack that is strapped to her body. With the eggs safely stowed, she winches herself back up to the top of the cliff.

Long after the humans have disappeared, the peregrines fly around and around, shrieking in distress: "*Cack cack cack cack.*"

A week or two later, the female has laid another three eggs. She is guarding them from intruders when her mate flies down to the nest, carrying a bird he has just killed. As the female takes the food and settles back on her eggs, she hears a faint crack. Two of the eggs have broken under the combined weight of the mother and her food.

The peregrines will raise only one chick themselves this year…but their first clutch of eggs will be raised by humans.

All over the land, birds were in trouble. For the past quarter century, small aircraft had sprayed farmers' fields with a pesticide called DDT.

DDT killed many harmful insects, but it also accumulated in the bodies of insect-eating birds. Birds of prey like the peregrine falcon, which ate the insect-eating birds, accumulated the most DDT of all.

DDT didn't kill birds of prey, but it made their eggshells so thin they broke easily. Many were unable to raise any chicks at all.

When people discovered what DDT had done to wildlife, a great protest movement began. Led by scientists and conservationists, ordinary people came together to fight for animal rights and the health of the environment. They succeeded in getting DDT banned.

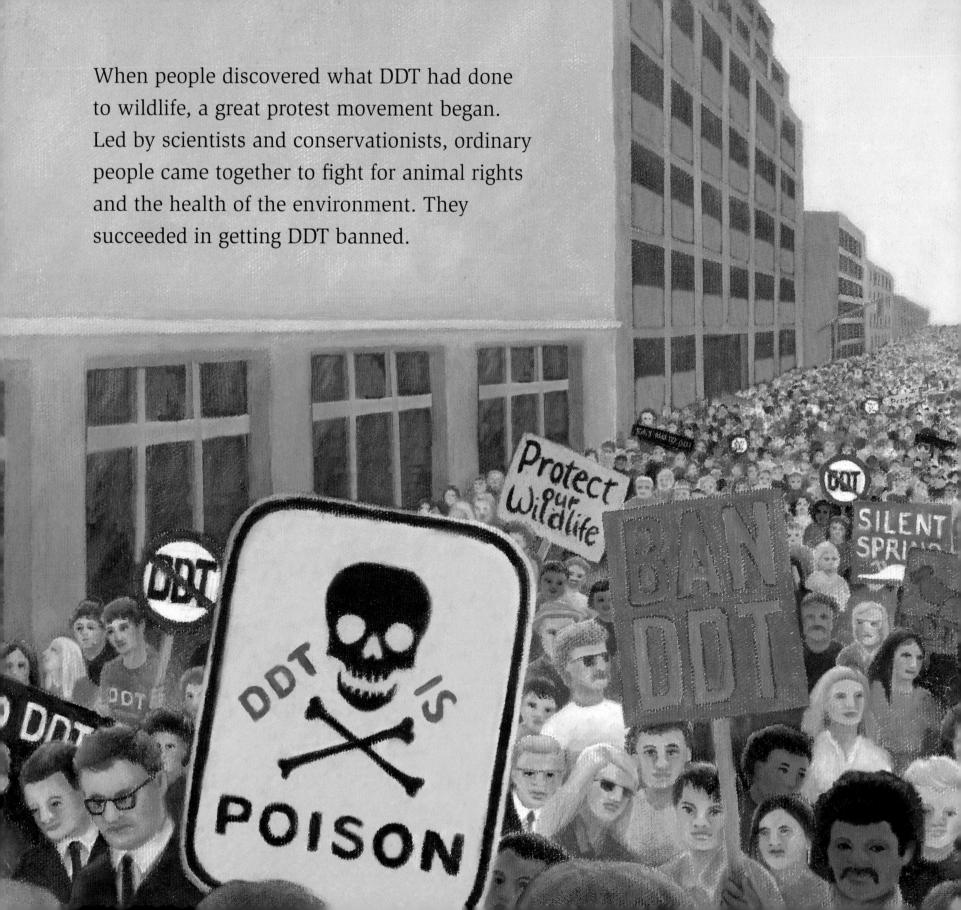

In the years following the ban on DDT, many bird populations began to recover. The peregrine falcon, however, had disappeared from great tracts of its former territory. To save this spectacular flyer—the fastest bird in the world—people had to make a special effort.

Bird experts and volunteers from all walks of life came from across the continent to help save this magnificent bird. One of them was the young woman who scaled the cliff to take that first clutch of eggs.

The falcon rescue teams know that peregrines often lay a second clutch if the first is destroyed. They hope the birds will raise more chicks.

The team takes the eggs to a sanctuary and places them in an incubator. In this warm, protected place, the fragile eggs have a better chance to survive. Sure enough, three weeks later, four downy chicks hatch into a strange new world.

One of the four hatchlings will be kept at the sanctuary and hand fed by her human captors.

When she is two years old, she will be paired with a captive male from a different nest. Over the years, in the safety of the sanctuary, she and her mate will raise brood after brood of chicks.

Some of her chicks will remain in captivity. Others will be released into the wild.

The other three hatchlings are kept from human contact so they won't become tame. They are fed through a hole in their nest box. After a few weeks, they are moved to a nest platform on the side of a cliff, where their food will be delivered through a tube that runs down the rock face.

Early one morning, as the sky is lightening in the east, a great horned owl is flying home to roost.

When a sleepy chick stirs in the nest, the owl's sharp eyes spot the movement. Silently, she sweeps down and plucks the chick from his perch.

The volunteer who feeds the chicks is saddened to discover that one of his nestlings has vanished in the night. He knows a great horned owl has most likely carried it off. There's a good chance the predator will return.

The volunteer calls the sanctuary staff. They decide to move the remaining two chicks to the city, where there are no great horned owls.

The chicks are placed on a ledge, high up on a skyscraper. They are fed dead pigeons, which are dropped down a feeding tube. Soon the volunteers observe the young falcons swooping and diving on live pigeons as they learn to hunt for themselves.

One of the two peregrines claims the skyscraper ledge for herself. She finds a mate and, in time, they raise a family of their own.

Her brother flies off in search of a mate. Perhaps he will return to the countryside to live wild and free. Perhaps he will stay in the city.

In spite of the many setbacks encountered by the peregrines and their human helpers, the peregrine rescue effort has been a success. Peregrine falcons can be seen once again soaring and diving in the skies, not only over their traditional wild territories, but in cities too.

Look up! Maybe there's one living near you.

Author's Note

How fast is the fastest bird in the world? Estimates vary, but one National Geographic team clocked a peregrine in a power dive at 242 miles (387 kilometers) an hour. Google "**National Geographic peregrine falcon**" to find the website's most current videos of the bird in action.

Another excellent source of images and information can be found at: **www.arkive.org** (enter "**peregrine falcon**" in the search box).

For more information on the peregrine rescue effort, visit:

- www.birds.cornell.edu/Publications/LivingBird/ summer99/missionaccomplished.html

- www.njfishandwildlife.net/artperegrine.htm

Though DDT is no longer used in Canada, the United States, or Europe, the use of pesticides in agriculture is increasing. New pesticides are constantly being developed; some may pose a threat to birds and other wildlife. It's thought, for example, that pesticides are responsible for the recent decline in bee populations. We must be vigilant to ensure that these new chemicals don't do more harm than good.

To learn more about rescue efforts for many different kinds of birds and to view a video of children enjoying a visit to a bird sanctuary, visit **www.peregrinefund.org**

For those fortunate enough to visit the West Coast, I highly recommend a trip to The Raptors in Duncan, B.C. Check out their website at **www.pnwraptors.com**